BENT FOR THE JOB

BENT FOR THE JOB
NEW POEMS

mick guffan

illustration by **Krent Able**

the tangerine press • london • 2021

ISBN 978-1-910691-72-4 (paperback)
      978-1-910691-73-1 (hardback)

BENT FOR THE JOB. COPYRIGHT © 2021 THE ESTATE OF MICK GUFFAN
ILLUSTRATION. COPYRIGHT © 2021 KRENT ABLE
THIS EDITION FIRST PUBLISHED 2021 BY TANGERINE PRESS
UNIT 18, RIVERSIDE ROAD
GARRATT BUSINESS PARK
LONDON
SW17 0BA
ENGLAND
thetangerinepress.com
PRINTED IN ENGLAND
ALL RIGHTS RESERVED

Tangerine Press books are printed on acid-free paper

ACKNOWLEDGEMENTS

THESE POEMS, many of which were discovered in Mick Guffan's flat shortly after his death in 2006, are finally together again, only this time not in tattered and torn sheets under the floorboards, but in book form.

The poems 'A Cage of Silk', 'Three Billion Less' and 'The Quiet Knock' first appeared in *River Dog*. Still more were first published in limited edition chapbooks by Tangerine Press, all now long out-of-print. The remainder have never before seen the light of day.

Respect and thanks are due to: Ruthie Wantling; Krent Able; Brian David Stevens; Alan Dent; Abbie Foxton; Salena Godden; James Kelman; Trevor Reeves; Jenni Fagan; John Dorsey; Tim Wells; Richard Goodley; Jeffrey Weinberg; Meena Kandasamy; Karina Bush; Billy Childish; Nick Lee; Steve Lowe; Benjamin Myers; Adelle Stripe; Ella Harrison; Saul Adamczewski; Lisa Cradduck; Danielle Quinn; Freya Beer; Thurston Moore; Mirella Sikorski; Fiona Betts; Pete, Ed and Poppy; Jonny Illingworth; Sophie Polyviou; Claudia Bierschenk; Andrew Mills; Jim Gibson; Sophie Pitchford; Sophie Cameron and Roger James Guffan (1975-93). The publisher wishes to extend an extra special thank you to the Guffan Clan for their continued support, patience and understanding.

— MICHAEL CURRAN

OTHER BOOKS BY MICK GUFFAN

Building the Quoins

Little Wars

Spoor Beast

Emoshun iz My Bizness

The Prickish Smell of Unwanted Cum: Love Poems

Inner London Buddha

Twenty Six Letters Scattered Sorted Loved & Unleashed

Cigarette Papers Through a Bottle

Stupor's Chain

The Bastard Brother

Inner London Buddha: Selected & Unpublished Poems 1999–2006

I am My Own Crew

The Sole of Discreshun

True to the Game

The Blahsted Nark★

Mick Guffan is a Bad Vibe★

The Quoin Fellow★

King of the Cockroaches★

The Master of Fuck All★

Modern Poetry for Private People★

★ *unpublished*

TABLE OF CONTENTS

Illustration xv

I

To the Reader 19

The Shining 20

Potted History 21

Minnie Riperton 22

Delectation 23

Bad Bad Talk 24

Corner of Carter and Creed 25

Alliance 26

Mick Guffan is Not Your Brother 27

Selfish 28

Clearly 29

Arrival 30

Busker 31

Get Carter 32

Option 33

Tooting Moon Goddess 34

Drag 35

Man Flooring 36

Rosie Lee Cafe Sketch 37

War and Peace 38

New Times 39

Did Cain Kill Abel? 40

Come on, Pilgrim 41

Wandering 42

Somniac 43

Of Angels and Dirt 44

Mixing Bowl 45

Hiding 46

Pillar to Post 47

To the Poet Who Threatened Suicide 48

Dream 49

Progress 50

Heyoka 51

Chin and Cheeks 52

Nothing More to be Said 53

II

One Short Poem 57

I Go to Better Beds 58

Success 59

A Visit to the Museum 60

Sombre Sunday 61

Next 62

Macho Sluts 63

No More 64

War Zone 65

3 Billion Less 66

Audience 67

Odd Coloured, Awkward & Heavy 68

Dusted Off 69

More or Less Communion 70

One Off 71

Husky Rescue 72

A Cage of Silk 73

Conversation 74

Afterthought 75

Short Story 76

Lame 77

The Machine Knows All Universes 78

The Quiet Knock 79

9.50am, Tuesday, Chatham 80

Slough, 1980 81

Weeds 82

Evening Star 83

"Most people are other people. Their thoughts are someone else's opinions, their lives a mimicry, their passions a quotation."

— Oscar Wilde

BENT FOR THE JOB
NEW POEMS

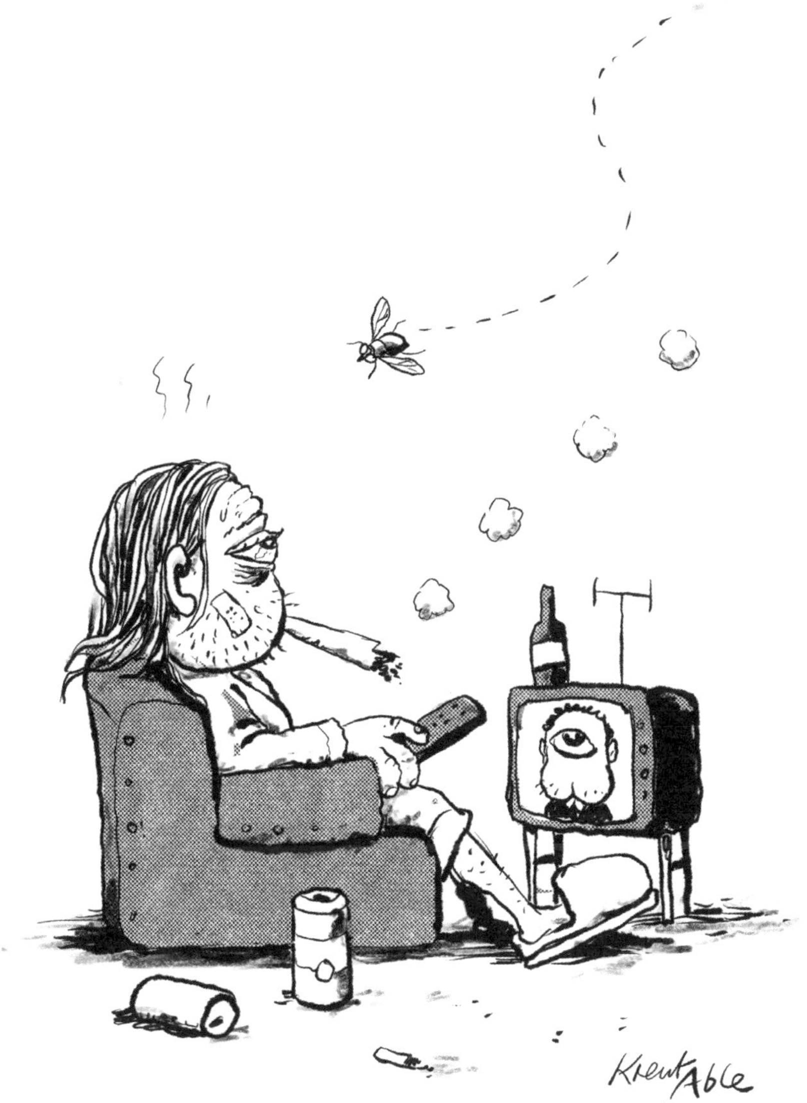
Krent Able
after
Philip Guston
2021

*It is the short
fuse
on a God Almighty
disease
that can
spark the
simplest of
pleasures*

TO THE READER

This figure, that you feast upon
it is the gentle Guffan—
where in his grief
and strife with nature
tries to outwit his style.
If he could have drawn it out
with good humour, as is his wont
only then would he surpass
all events so brief.
But, since he cannot, dear Reader
look no further upon this poem
but this book.

THE SHINING

There's this one scene that stands out.
Your man Jack—
table-slumped
in the middle of a
bad dream
in the middle of the
Colorado Lounge;
awakened by Wendy, snapping
him out of it.
Slowly, Danny appears
shuffling quietly—
Wendy looks up
runs to her son.
There's this bruising around the neck
a torn collar.
She's going over it in her mind
fretting, hysterical...
holds Danny close, backing away:
You did this to him
How could you
How could you

POTTED HISTORY

At first I thought
they were scars—
actually furrows, on
a brow.

Kept that to myself.

Not a happy face
as it turned out.

MINNIE RIPERTON

I love the way sisters
looked in those days.
No weaves, no make up, no tats everywhere
no fakery, no injections.
No grafted devils.

DELECTATION

I want to shake off this habit.
Maybe flirt with a cliché—
stand naked in front of a mirror.
Shed my grief-skin.
But it's the hagridden
dreams in daylight
calling the shots—
and those without shade
never
see the sun.

BAD BAD TALK

She pours this stuff out—
I tilt my head
listening to
bad bad talk
listening
shaking my head
saying no no
you're wrong
no
I don't believe you
and wouldn't you know
this huge ball of salty glycerine
appears
drops like sorrow
onto the carpet
and she laughs at
her power over me
(and so do I)
then carries
on with her
bad bad talk
my heart a drunken
god of the morning
and eyes now dry

CORNER OF CARTER AND CREED

I am not in the gutter—
that is where I throw
my blunts

ALLIANCE

My neighbour and I
are laughing.
At different things
but it is
laughter nonetheless.

We have been here before—
Torchlight, paper, radio.

My neighbour is laughing
louder now
as I whisper yes to a secret
kept from childhood.

MICK GUFFAN IS NOT YOUR BROTHER

You do not know me, I am faceless.
A bad player
despite the beauty, the sentiments.
I am not your brother.
I have no thread, sinew or fluid.
Moral gymnastics are tiring.
Look carefully, look closely.
You will find me by the counter—
a contented machine
nodding and
listening
til I am charged.

SELFISH

After I heard
I began to think of
all the little feelings
over the years—
of something
growing
inside me
uninvited.
Heading for all the
vital areas
restricting me
smothering me
hindering all actions
diminishing them
halving them—
becoming less possible
and
yet more magical.

CLEARLY

Living to see clearly—
I do not need this jacket
these shirts
trousers
or shoes.
Shelley, Bronte, all that gang—
those fuckers never
had a clue.
Yes, my friends
it is fun
to watch yourself burn.

ARRIVAL

A fly has just landed
on my head.
Fat, lazy, tickly
sludging around the
sweat, hair and skin.
It's a big world.

BUSKER

I think his name is John
(a safe bet)
and he is strumming
some popular tune.
Children cry when they
look at him.
Inside, ohming
with pain.
I mean:
O H M
you know?
I try that—
a divine thing
ohming with this busker.
A shitty, buddhist hi-jacking.
He is not going anywhere.

GET CARTER

I forget when—
maybe around the middle of the action.
It's where your man Jack
appears at the bottom of the stairs.
Walking up slowly, he says:
Tell me about the girl.
Then, kind of simmering
he's standing over Glenda.
She's in the bath and acting vague, of course.
Still, he won't have it, grabs her by the hair
dunks then fishes her out.
He's right in her face, but not like before:
Now
Tell me the truth

OPTION

In the event of
enthusiasm
being an option
she said, why don't you?
Maybe it will help.
I stopped doing what I was doing.
She took my hand, steered it.
I felt angry
but had to stay.
No bolthole
not even that.

TOOTING MOON GODDESS

After storing it in thirteen jars
under the stairs
(all the time, I've known)
she wants to try this—
so, one afternoon, we
give it a go.
Standing astride
(me supine)
on creased bedsheets
her menses
dropping onto my grateful
belly.
That flow
smells different somehow
and, dabbing my finger—
not the usual
aftertaste.
Looking down at me, she says:
You're no good, Mick.
Really?
I reply.

DRAG

Weighing up the
pros and cons
of eugenics.
Thinking of European cities
beginning with the letter D.
Considering the social life
of insects.
Patiently interviewing global leaders
with my imagination
intact.
Thank you.
I am now ready
for the full price ticket
to a show downstairs.
Dante is on the bill, apparently.
A rare appearance.
No interval.

MAN FLOORING

The
Nights
Walk
Home
Like
Tame
Mares
Through
Tunnels

Groundless
Optimism

ROSIE LEE CAFE SKETCH: SCAFFOLD BOSS ON PHONE, 11AM

This was how I found him, in the cafe, pacing about:

He says, the three of you, he doesn't want you back on site.

Because you're being abusive. Ozzie bastards and all that.

I'm not interested. That's what he's told me, now I'm telling you.

Okay, yeah, okay.

Hangs up, redials.

I've spoken to Buck. He's denying it.

Well, look, I'll give you his number. Sort it out amongst yourselves.

Number.

He's saying it's not him.

Yeah, Buck's passing the buck.

Bucknell.

Okay, yeah, okay.

Hangs up. Redials. Thinks better of it and hangs up again.

Walks to the counter:

Two bacon rolls to take away, please.

No sauce.

WAR AND PEACE

I am my own war.
That cordier got it.
Long gone on a late night tube train.
We were close—
forced, but not
(if you get my meaning).
Heading, no doubt, to the end of whatever line:
You got kind eyes, brother.
I was 26 years of age.
It was the most beautiful thing
anyone ever said
to me.

NEW TIMES

I put it down.

You laugh
picking it up.

Treat me like shit.

But I do not want
to smell and be pastey.

I blow pubic hair
from the table.

Never clean up.

Lighting candles
while you chant.

My turn to laugh.

At last, I treat you
like the smelly, pastey
stuff you so adore.

DID CAIN KILL ABEL?

Warm cunt, cold bitch
next to me.
I pivot on my arse carefully
so as not to disturb her.
Everything hurts as I
cut my hair with a
Kabar hunting knife.
These whiskers teeming with lice—
I leave them well alone.
What do you think of the new haircut?
I ask, re-entering the bedroom.
(Nothing I say
surprises her
anymore)
She looks over her white shoulder and says:
Please use your knees
to pick up your feet cos
this novel won't write itself

COME ON, PILGRIM

You can dig—
you can dig, dig
some more.
These pilgrims are crazy like foxes.
Their last idiocy is
sombre, indigo
an orphan.
But it just takes one to kow-tow, very easily
then the rest of em.
So I say:
thanks for that
close the window
enjoy the last
idiotic drink
alone
in a darkened room.
Now, who's up for an adventure?

WANDERING

I have been without a woman
so long
I walk behind them.
No, not like that.
Downwind only.
To catch a sense—
take it in, deeply.
And what do I offer in
return?
Balls swinging with bad sperm
stale breath
and a pickled gherkin.

SOMNIAC

and you squeeze your eyes shut
til they sink and surge
so much a
glycerine mouse
trickles into
your ear—
...letting go...
but cannot cos it's
cunts like you that
make living so difficult

OF ANGELS AND DIRT

fall, fail—
only
to hurt again

MIXING BOWL

Earliest memory:
Stuffing my cakehole—
spoonfuls from mother's sickly mix.
A chocolate explosion across my face.
Puked after.

HIDING

Another one:
Calling mother a COW—
she squealed to father, of course
and my hiding beneath the
ironing board
amongst creased shirts and bedsheets;
the old man charging in—
pinned down and
giving me what for
over and
over and
mother
watching

PILLAR TO POST

And again:
My brothers—
using me like a
ragged doll.
Two years old.
Back garden.
Them: very dark, very bright.
Me: strawberry blonde
black and blue and
trying
to
get
away

TO THE POET WHO THREATENED SUICIDE

Go ahead, you useless little shit.
Your writing weren't never any
good anyway.

DREAM

For once—
getting precious
explaining a poem
and you nodding
backing
away

PROGRESS

Maybe I should write one of
them   clever
    poems
with
words that   jump
              about
and yes perhaps some   considered.punctuation
so
    you
        will
  look
for   (hiDDen)
       meanings
           think.I.am.
   cleverer
than what I.really.am
       yes maybe   that   will
tick / some / boxes
merit an   Arse Council   handout
or get me in *Rialto, Magma*
Poetry Now
            or even
simply make you
     cum   cum   cum

HEYOKA

A familiar routine.
Unloading tools from the van
piling them up
in the understairs cupboard.
Analogue meters purr there.
But it's the gas digits that get my attention—
four in white, two in red.
White was one, nine, six and nine
Red was five and three.

Then a picture appears
of a ten year old boy—
me when young.
Eyes adjusting
tracing the frame.

I ignore all this
move gracefully into the kitchen
get the rice on
whilst I clean my favourite bowl.
Leaning over, staring into boiling water
only to see Rebecca West—
she smiles at me
then disappears.

Outside a dog barks
seeming satisfied.

CHIN AND CHEEKS

Not quite at the back.
One or two rows
forward, I would say.
They always found me.
A fucking magnet for it!
Wow, yes
that red-faced, yellow-shirted
brown-tied bastard—
him, especially.
I'd be working on a finger pot or
whatever.
A bunch of keys fly past.
Then a board duster from nowhere hits my chest
with a puff of chalk, slo-mo
Peckinpah-style.
Then old clay breath was right
on me:
WHEN *WILL* YOU START SHAVING, GUFFAN?!
Those words made my
face as red as his.
Then he grabbed my hair and
SMACK
SMACK
on the edge of the desk.
Looking up with a slit ridge across my dizzy forehead
all eyes turned
settle below mine
staring at the shameful fluff
on my
chin and cheeks.

NOTHING MORE TO BE SAID

I read these poems and
decide I am not fooling anyone—
that they are the mind-puke of a perfumed whore and
the titles are better than
what follows

*Adjust the noose
like collar and tie:
Now we are ready*

ONE SHORT POEM

I do not know where it all went wrong.
Perhaps it was never right.
Father penetrated Mother.
Then?
Nah, too easy.

I GO TO BETTER BEDS

To put it short—
My shit is like a fat, beef-brown worm
gripped in an arse-like vice.
Fingers securely locked behind
my sweaty head.
A stained pillowcase completes the scene.
I know what is coming.
You couldn't make it up.
Here she is, marching up the stairs.
I can hear her now:
Just give me a reason, Mick
one good reason
why I should stay

SUCCESS

Cash rules everything around me, so
I ask:
Is the man done?
Then, I am heavy in a limousine.

A VISIT TO THE MUSEUM

Browsing the bottom shelf
three specimen jars in a row.
Antiquated floating pricks as pathologist reference—
near an exposed, dangling double socket.
A sign below them all saying:
"Faulty, do not use."

SOMBRE SUNDAY

Act polite.
Be a piglet
safe in bed.

Soak up a knowledgable, deep
small book
taking on
the bigger picture.

Laugh at medicines
having been so good
for so long and yes
now laughable.

Get up—
march for miles to release those fears
but you still throw up after sex.

NEXT

Well, what do you
know?
A spider has just
given out
on the stairs.
(I struggle too
but my victory is phoney)
I pick it up, place it in a safety
deposit box.
Under the stairs
with all those jars.
What next—get drunk, get closer to it?
Nah; I put the kettle on
turn out the lights
say quietly to nothing and no-one in particular:
Let me love in my own way

MACHO SLUTS

You know the ones—
kissing Mother's neck
in front of Father
(great poem)
and hating
their sisters
for those silly swinging breasts

NO MORE

Having wasted
my time
here comes the
salt and warm water.

I jump at the noise
of a football against
a wall.

I pour long life
milk down the sink
(I have no fridge).

Roses bought in haste
now droop over low Edwardian walls.

I am emphatically
disinterested
in learning any
more secrets.

WAR ZONE

guns like drum rolls
that
smoke away the evidence—
my
arms too short to box with God

3 BILLION LESS

The older I get
the more I want to return
to that time.
My life
was free—
rolling fat ones
for my brothers
(an outrageous solstice
beckoning)
Father drinking
in his cold cabin
(a death so unexpected
waiting)
and there were
3 billion less people on the planet.

AUDIENCE

I was behind them when
the overweight, older woman
parked herself on a low wall
dropping two overloaded bags with a sulky *thump*.

The men carried on
walking and talking.

As I drew level with her
the men stopped and turned round.

I wanted to see if you
remembered that there were
three people going shopping and
not *two!* she said.

As I passed through their crisis
she told them to
oh . . . fuck off in a tired way.

The men looked at each other.

I continued forward
a naked notepad left open at home.

A woman looking over it
who should not.

ODD COLOURED, AWKWARD & HEAVY

Well, for a start it is purple
fills up half the room and is in
the way permanently.

I have tried leaning it against the wall
in different corners—
doesn't help.

I have considered selling it
but at the moment
it makes a very
useful footrest.

When I lie on the floor
it becomes a very useful
headrest.

It is heavy
8 foot long
awkward to grip
the girth is 12 inches or so—
it is also very slippy.

It cost me £105 and I cannot
get rid of it.

I have offered it to friends
for half its value but no-one wants it.

I am lost.
I am at my wit's end.

DUSTED OFF

I was sweeping up as he pulled over.
Walking straight past me
he checked the kitchen door.
I followed him back outside, into the van.
He turned off his phone
rested it on the dashboard:
Mick, how do you feel it's all going?
The windows were beginning to steam up.
Protocol or civilization or three weeks of unpaid wages
kept me in that van like a rusty vice.
No hard feelings, he said and
offered his hand.
An old habit—
wiping the mist
from the windscreen.
Don't worry about that, he said, switching his phone back on.
It always steams up in here.

MORE OR LESS COMMUNION

In my current state of mind
perhaps it is best
to be my own crew—
cos no matter
where I go
what I see
hear or
read
they keep
telling us
telling us.

I do not listen
to God like that.

ONE OFF

Mother and child
approach

The boy
runs his toy
car
along a
wall

steps over my legs
catches my eye

The Right Height

HUSKY RESCUE

How to start all this?
With grease on my fingertips
I could name a day.
But that would upset you.
The length of time, I mean.
From then til now.
You could be kind and say
it is unusual.
We both know why.
The others taught themselves to turn away.
I still feel their horror.
Looking across at the shaped glass on the table
I note one set of fingerprints.
So as not to confuse you—
there's that grease again.
Several times.
Am I a robot? What am I?

A CAGE OF SILK

Drop-stitch—
a cage of silk around my bed.
Mere 'mind-forged manacles'
laughed at by the gods.
(Only the righteous
shall be saved)
Ah yes, all in good time.
There are
so many
different
people to be.

CONVERSATION

Looking out across the wet edition of streets, I tried (and failed)
to coax a sonic boom of stories—
the being one of eight
the throwing of a single slice
of bread into the shoeless crowd of them
and their mother screaming:
That's all there is!
The fairground bouts for pennies
training at The Ring, Blackfriars
the pro tour, Berlin, 1936
(See that suitcase? Been in front of Hitler)
going the distance with Freddie Mills, Brighton Aquarium, 1938
the lying, the cheating, the falling fists and the failing heart
Part of that trying was
the
sniffing around
shoeboxes
biscuit tins
bezoar memories
and after all that
(the false starts
and let's face it
a final lack of conviction)
Thomas Frank Guffan says:
Perhaps he's afraid of what he
might find

AFTERTHOUGHT

The night was a shameful arousal.
Propped me up like a sex toy.
(You check your watch
tie both my hands…)

Door-click.
Downstairs—
the kitchen is here
the hallway there.
Thin walls are just that.
I masturbate while
the kettle boils
stir semen
into my coffee
add dandelion syrup to taste.
Legs now like clumsy armadillos.
The letting go, the sadness of sex.
No matter.
I will pay for it Monday.

SHORT STORY

I push down the keys, they return.
Arms around my neck—
I struggle
then relax.

How's it going?

Terrible.

We stare at the screen.
God, bohemia is far from here.

LAME

He is in a chair
cos he has to be
He is nicer than before
cos he has to be . . .
Nah, hold on—
Wantling said it better:
'Kind only when frightened
Humble only in pain.'
That's it.

THE MACHINE KNOWS ALL UNIVERSES

No more *NOW* no more *THEN*
This seeker
of visions
is swarming with concessions

THE QUIET KNOCK

It's hard to explain. Dreams like diagrams. Ha! What does *that* mean? Really detailed. Umm. Tight and symetrical. Wow . . . not things, not people — just detailed diagrams. Make any sense? Hmmm. It's the exactness, sharpness I remember. Vast microchipscapes is the nearest I can get. Colour? Don't think so. None that I recall. The only other time I dreamt like that — y'know, out of form or whatever — was in cartoon. Yes, cartoon. Years ago. People I knew, didn't know, domestic scenes. Street scenes. Talking. Moving about. Very fluid, natural. But everything was in cartoon. Crazy. That was a one off though. The detailed diagram stuff went on for a while. Then went.

9.50AM, TUESDAY, CHATHAM

A pleasant breakfast ruined by an
electric-blue-haired
red-faced lady
screaming, kicking
at a front door.
Ground floor window
a man leans out.
She goes for his throat.
Another man, burly, forthright
(fancies himself as cavalry)
crosses the
road, grabs her other arm
(Child's writing — further down —
another unpolished window
After Every Storm Comes a Rainbow)
A police siren.
The sun pushes its face out.
She rips the window man's t-shirt
(revealing an indifferent nipple)
the burly man
pulls at her arm, pleading.
She is on a rack of sorts
no sum, no angle
yet oddly and wildly
in control
of the whole fucking universe.

SLOUGH, 1980

We would slope down the stairs
peer in and there they were
through the glass.
A man and a woman in the front room.
Quiet, thoughtful.
My friend and I stifle-laughed
like the cowards we were.
We could not hear it but found out
later they would sit and listen to classical music together
like this
for hours.
Fast forward the years and
here
I am listening to Bruckner's
Symphony No. 7 in E Major
a glass of putrid wine
a slice of warm cheese
circled by
endless errors
countless, goading, chiding, beyond everything—
still unspoken
those two adults now
long
gone to
earth.

WEEDS

That's right.
Garden weeds.
Wait til everyone was out of site
busy in the kitchen—
elsewhere, in other words.

The good stuff was round the side.
All virile, damp and alive, like.
Some offered resistance, me
tugging and tearing handfuls
and munching away like some kind of
mad little lost monkey—
Chew, swallow, look around.
Like in the tv programmes.
Dryness hit my mouth and yuck.
So it was a sneak into the
front room.
The Drinks Cabinet.
I knew where the key was.
Bottles clunk lazily aside as I pull out
then start on the tonic water.
I had seen the adults use it.
I washed away the dry with wet-dry.
Why was it Indian?
That didn't make any sense.
Fizzy water from India?

Looking back
that was one healthy diet
for a six year old.

EVENING STAR

I vow never to touch
my penis again
(expect to piss)
read my Bible
every afternoon
preach sermons on love
tackle all demons
as they reveal themselves
become a master of
the evening star
accept anything my betters
tell me
and if you find this
inconsistent or
difficult to believe
I cannot help you

Mick Guffan (1953-2006) was born in An Sciobairín, Cork, Ireland, the youngest of five brothers. He came to England at the age of 18, working variously as a taxi driver, airplane cleaner and finally as a carpenter. He died at St. George's Hospital, Tooting, London on 14th June 2006, his body set about by nervous exhaustion following an altercation in a nearby public house.

Krent Able is a comic artist and illustrator, living in London. His books include *Krent Able's Big Book of Mischief* and *The Second Coming of Krent Able*, and he has co-written the award-winning films *Ink, Cocks & Rock 'n' Roll* and *Deep Clean*, and co-edited the graphic anthologies *I FEEL MACHINE* and *I FEEL LOVE*. His work has appeared in *The Guardian, Vice* and *The NME*, and was featured in the Comics Unmasked exhibition at The British Library in 2014. He also works as a storyboard and concept artist for clients such as Disney, Universal Pictures and Danny Boyle.

May 2021

This first edition is published as a trade paperback; there are 50 numbered copies signed by the illustrator & publisher, & handbound in boards by the Tangerine Press, Tooting, London; numbered copies also contain additional artwork by Krent Able.